# Farming's Fantastic Facts

**Rena Buck Will**

# — A MAVERICK PUBLICATION —

# Table of Contents

# Acknowledgements

A very big thank you to each grower who read and approved the way in which I depicted his specific area of agriculture. Thanks to everyone who helped in any way.

"There is a definite need in Oregon and other states for relevant, usable and meaningful reference materials as aids in integrating agriculture into the classroom.

*Farming's Fantastic Facts* would serve that need, and would be a valuable addition to a school library.

In the area of constructive observation of the work, one recommendation might be to develop one version for the younger student and retain the thrust of the current manuscript as an aid for the higher elementary grades.

The basic material for a good reference book is there."

Ray Hobson, Assitant Director
Department of Agriculture
State of Oregon

"A good overview of agriculture in the United States. This book is the first serious book about farming which I have seen for elementary school pupils. I cheer this effort to provide information at this level as we attempt to expose our pupils to the many career choices which are available."

Robert R. Ditmer
Principal
Dayton Public Schools

•••

"It's heartening to read a book written for a primary grade school children that tells about agriculture, its beginnings, its importance and its way of life. In this day when such a high percentage of our young people grow up in cities and do not have the opportunity for a farm experience, it is good to have a book that may be useful in teaching them about the science of farming and its way of life."

Sincerely,
Wayne Roberts
Extension Agent

•••

"I feel the book accurately portrays the many aspects of agriculture. It would be an excellent resource tool in the education of elementary students.

Too, it has potential for being converted to a textbook for use in conjunction with physical and social science classes. In this manner in-classroom activities complimenting reading assignments would create student interest.

The book is of a broad enough base that it could be used at very young age or with junior high students."

Matthew S. Weimar
Agricultural Resource Coordinator
Oregon State Department of Agriculture

**Dedicated to**

*boys and girls wanting to learn more about their food and its sources. It is also dedicated to the farmers who supply that food.*

The aim of this book is to present to young people of the United States a brief summary on agriculture and what it means to them.

# Chapter I

# Farming

Farming goes back a long way in our history, even into pre-history. In Bat Cave, New Mexico, archaeologists have found primitive corn and Indian tools some five thousand years old.

Then in a Tehuacan Valley Cave south of Mexico City an American archaeologist discovered the link between the wild corn and the corn of today. He not only found wild corn plants dating back to between 5200 and 3400 B.C. but, continuing on in later layers at the same dig, he found the ears were progessively larger. This indicated the Indians planted, cultivated and propagated corn in sufficient quantities to supply a staple food. It was learned they even had a surplus for trade. By around 2500 B.C., in addition to the corn, these people were growing patches of many plants native to the Americas. These were called cultigens and included beans, squash, avocados and chili peppers.

By 1500 B.C. knowledge of this corn cultivation, as well as that of other food crops, had spread throughout the area. Also the knowledge of cotton and how to cultivate it and transform its fiber into cloth had spread. The people gathered and became semi-settled farmers.

Some of these same people migrated to our own southwest about 300 or 400 B.C. They brought with them the means for survival including the cultigens and the know-how to irrigate.

Unearthed Indian villages have disclosed corn and squash seed stored in pottery jars awaiting time for planting the next crop.

In the Bible there are many references to farming. The people of that day seem to have been doing a fair job of feeding themselves by farming.

Today, farming is sometimes called a science. There are those who say farming is an art, yet others say it is more of a feeling. The theory in this book is that farming is some of all three. The methods used in the many operations depend on the farmer who is doing the job.

Farming has more variables or changing factors than most businesses. It *is* a business, but it is much much more. There is no truer slogan than, "If you eat, you are involved with agriculture." That seems to cover almost everyone.

There are variables in the amount of sunshine during the season. How many hot days will there be? Will there be enough water to irrigate when the corp needs it? How will hail, cold wind, or cool cloudy mornings affect the germination or seed sprouting, the stand and the growth? If he has river-bottom land, the farmer has another concern. Does the river flood and what time does this generally occur? These are some of the factors the farmer must consider before planting time.

But there has never been a satisfactory way of feeding the nation without farming. So you see you *are* involved with agriculture—you depend on it for your food!

It is sometimes hard to wait for the strawberries to get ripe.

Blackberries that have been trained for next year's crop.

A large crew harvesting broccoli.

Green bean picker in action.

Green bean harvest.

Planting broccoli.

Loading boysenberries to haul to the cannery.

A bean just peeking through the ground.

Walnuts still in their green husks.

Budding varieties onto
seedling apple trees.

Different scenes of tilling.

Sugar cane, with tassles.

Sweet corn field.

New sugar cane field.

Peaches ready to pick.

Straw remains after harvesting grain.

*Chapter II*

# Climate, Soils and Tilling

## Climate

The climate has a distinct bearing on the crops grown in a specific area. Each crop has its number of days consisting of a certain number of heat units that are required to raise a crop and produce a good harvest.

If a farmer plants a long growing crop in a short growing climate, the cold weather arrives before the crop is mature and ready for harvest. When that happens, he will have no harvest and will be in economic trouble on that crop. Or perhaps the area is subject to having freezing nights during the growing season. This also spells disaster for many crops. Some crops are killed by just one freezing night. Or perhaps the freeze comes when the plant is blooming and kills the potential fruit.

The same applies to a crop which needs a certain amount of sun, but not too much high humidity, or damp weather. Some crops are affected by a disease called blight when the weather is too damp for them. Their leaves turn dark and the fruit rots rapidly.

Blight is infectious, and spreads from one plant or product to another. Potatoes and tomatoes are among those that are very susceptible and sensitive to blight in warm damp weather. Some orchards and fruit also get blight. Blight causes great fruit losses. A farmer has to know which crop will withstand more cold, heat, wet conditions, and dry seasons if he is to be successful at farming.

## Soils

Although farming soils range from 90% sand to 90% clay, to make things simple in this book we are classifying soils into four groups. Here we are calling the types sandy, clay, acid and alkali. We will refer to sandy as a light soil and clay as a heavy soil.

The sandy soils are especially good for root crops such as potatoes, carrots, and beets. The sand tends to turn out a smoother product. Grass and pasture do well on heavier soil. If a farmer has cattle and some heavy soil and some lighter ground, he will most likely plant pasture on the heavier type. This will free the lighter soil for growing other crops. The sandy soil holds water for a shorter period, and will require more water to prevent the crop from suffering from thirst. Some sandy soils drink water so fast that one gets the feeling there is no bottom.

Grass helps heavier soil. Grass has a root system which spreads extensively, and penetrates the ground, allowing the excess water to escape. One can help heavy soil by growing a thick cover crop during the fall and winter. In the spring the cover

Preparing the soil for planting.

Plowing turns the grass under and starts breaking up the soil for a new crop.

After plowing the soil is disked and harrowed.

crop is turned under and rots. This adds humus to the soil and returns nutrients (food) into the ground. This helps the following year's crops. Alfalfa is used to improve heavy soil. It is a broad leaf plant that is used for hay, or added to other feed. It has a long tap root which is good to penetrate the clay and make a passageway for aeration and drainage. Earth worms also improve the soil by making little tunnels in the ground and loosening it for freer plant growth. One of the most helpful things to do for heavy soil is to tile it by trenching a network of drainage tile in the ground below the plowing depth. The tile permits excess water to drain off and prepares the ground for growing many crops. Rotating the crops, planting a different crop on a field than was there last season, also helps.

The farmer adds lime to his acid soil to neutralize it in order to grow a profitable crop. After the liming process, the soil will grow a variety of crops.

Sulphur, or gypsum, is used to neutralize alkali soil and make it practical for many crops.

**Tilling**

Tilling is a method of stirring the soil and preparing a seed-bed or plant-bed for the crop. Tilling methods differ for different crops. They also vary from one farmer to another. A plow, disc, harrow, drag, and tiller are some of the tillage equipment. In some soils where the soil is heavier, or where it has been worked for a long time without relief, a chisel is used to penetrate the hard layer beneath the tillage area. Cutting this hard-pan allows the water to drain on down and avoid drowning the crop with wet roots. Plants are living things and can be drowned if they do not have proper ventilation. The amount of breathing required differs from one crop to another.

When the soil is worked into small particles, it allows a root crop to grow smoother bulbs, or product. But, a heavy rain or irrigation will seal off the air by forming a crust on top of the ground.

Tilled heavy clay soils have two problems. The top dries out from the porous surface, and within the growing area the ground remains too wet. It is difficult to maintain the proper moisture content in the soil. It is hard to have the soil damp enough to germinate the seed evenly. The clods are rock-like and make  planting difficult. Some parts are wet, while others are too dry. Seed needs a warm, moist bed in which to germinate. If the ground is too wet, the seed will rot or will not grow much after sprouting. But if it is dry and the grower irrigates to help germination and there is a shower of rain, then he is in trouble again. The top may be just right, but the ground beneath the surface will be saturated, because there is no escape for the water.

In areas where there is a lot of wind, a farmer does the least amount of stirring possible to produce a good crop. When the ground is loose, with nothing holding it down, the wind blows it away.

Some orchard crops need no tilling. There is mostly a native ground cover which is flailed or mowed frequently. By doing this, the ground remains level for easier mechanical harvest. If the vegetation is mowed often, it will not rob the crop of needed moisture. When it is time to till, the farmer weighs all these factors. Then he tills in a manner to suit his particular needs.

# Chapter III

# Planting and Fertilizing

## Planting

There are many ways of planting crops. Wheat, oats, rye, barley and other grains and grasses are planted with a planter called a grain drill. This drill is a wide seed box with metered tubes to make rows from one to nine inches apart. These tubes drop the seed into the ground from one-half to two inches apart. The seed spacing depends on the amount of seed the farmer feels his soil will be capable of sprouting and growing profitably. The grain drill also has a fertilizer hopper to place nutrients in the ground to feed the grain as it grows. When the grain is a foot high it covers the ground. These crops are usually planted in the fall. They withstand winter quite well in most farming areas. A period of dormancy helps the grains produce a better seed crop.

Beans, corn, carrots, beets, and many other vegetables are planted with planters that can seed several rows at a time. The rows for these are much wider than for grain. These planters have individual planter hoppers for each row. The planters also have fertilizer hoppers that put fertilizer into the ground on each side of the row of seed. The rows are adjusted far enough apart to permit tractors to operate within the spaces between the rows without damaging the crop. There will be tractors going through the fields to cultivate, fertilize, or spray. There will also need to be room for irrigation. In climates where there are four distinct seasons, these crops are planted in the spring.

Small plants are used for crops such as cane berries, strawberries, tomatoes, and cauliflower. Cabbage and broccoli are sometimes started by planting seed. Sometimes they are planted as small plants. If they are seeded, they have to be thinned later when the plants are large enough to ensure a good stand after thinning. These plants are planted with a machine which drops them into the ground and pulls the soil around them. This is usually done four rows at a time. Two people ride along side each hopper and help plants drop at the proper time. The plants are usually bought from a nursery which grows them in a greenhouse or a special field for that purpose. These crops are primarily planted in the spring.

Potatoes are planted differently. The potato itself is used to plant a new crop. There are eyes, or buds, on the potato which sprout and grow plants. The potato is cut into two to six pieces, depending on the size of the potato and the number of eyes. Of course, the piece must be large enough to furnish food for the new sprouted plant. The potato pieces are planted with a planter very similar to the corn planter, but it is adjusted to handle larger pieces and drop at different spacing. Fertilizer is placed in the ground along side the row to give the new plants a good start. Potatoes require a long growing season and are planted in early spring. Their leaves are easily nipped by late spring frost. Much like potatoes, sugar cane itself is planted. The eyes or joints produce new plants for the crop.

Fruit and nut orchards are planted with small tree plants called seedlings. Most of these are not true to any variety and must be grafted, or budded, with grafts or buds from older trees to get the desired variety of fruit. People have been working on improving the quality and eye-appeal and have succeeded in getting fruits and nuts that are superior to seedlings. Trees grow to be very large, and the spacing has to be correct for them to have room for their growth. They are usually planted far enough apart for the adult trees to get sunshine and air circulation around them.

Orchard and vineyard crops last many years. So, instead of planting every year, the farmer spends the off-season time pruning his trees and vines. Cane and trailing berries usually have a productive life of six to twelve years and are left in the fields for that time. The old canes and vines must be removed annually. This is sometimes done in the late summer or early fall after harvest. Other farmers prefer to do it in the winter months. The trailing vines are trained around wires stretched between posts. This

**Planting and fertilizing with the same machine.**

**Planting young plants for the next crop of broccoli.**

spreads the vines over a large area. It keeps them off the ground, and exposes the berries to enable people to pick them easier. The cane berries also need some support to keep them standing upright.

Strawberries usually bear fruit profitably for two to three years. They send out runners which root down and produce new plants. The farmer usually takes the runners off before they root into the ground. Some farmers prefer leaving these runners, but pushing them back into the row area and permitting the rows to get wider.

These are some of the things the farmers do to crops that are not planted every year.

**Fertilizer**

Fertilizer nutrients are blended together in the amounts that are needed for specific crops in different soils. The most common nutrients added are nitrogen, phosphorus, potassium, sulfur, and many other trace elements. These elements occur in the ground naturally, but not always in the proper amounts to grow a good crop. The crops require varying quantities of these elements to grow and produce a harvest. The plants take the nutrients out of the ground, so the farmer needs to replace them to keep his soil fertile and in good condition.

# Chapter IV

# Cultivation and Irrigation

Cultivation is stirring and loosening the ground. In some early history we find that people used sticks and bones to cultivate, or even make the hole to plant their seed. The American Indians broke rocks so there would be a sharp cutting edge. They used these as tools when cutting or digging. Since that time we have improved on their tools and methods.

There are three reasons for cultivation. One is to retain or keep the existing moisture in the soil. Another is to rid the ground of the weeds that have appeared since the farmer last worked the soil. The other reason is to aerate the soil and permit the plants to breathe.

The depth of cultivation depends on the crop being grown. The amount of cultivation depends on the farmer and the methods he uses to keep his ground and crop in good condition.

There are various ways with different machines used for cultivating crops. Sometimes a farmer uses a tractor to pull a cultivator which has shovels or small plows. These various shaped shovels stir the

One form of irrigation uses a gun like this.

A nurseryman cultivating young apple trees.

soil along side the plants and between the rows. Sometimes he uses a tiller with rotating teeth to loosen the soil and take out the young weeds. The tillers are set up with some teeth removed so they will straddle the rows and only work the middles, or furrows. Some farmers feel they can do well with less mechanical cultivation than they once felt was necessary to produce a good crop. Then there are crops and times when nothing takes the place of a hoe. A lot of handwork is required to remove weeds with a hoe. Working the ground with a machine can sometimes be omitted by using a chemical to remove the young weeds. This saves valuable time and expense, and eliminates packing the ground with so many wheel tracks. A ground sprayer covers much more area than a cultivator, so the field can be sprayed without leaving so many compacted streaks through the field. The sprays can also be applied by aircraft. Then there will be no ground disturbance at all.

## Irrigation

Water is essential to all living things. Irrigation is not new in this country. The Indians of the southwest two thousand years ago were growing corn, beans, and squash by leading water from the rivers to the crops through a network of canals. One of the finest and oldest waterways is three miles long and 2,300 years old. It is near Phoenix, Arizona. It was carved by the Hohokam Indians, using pointed sticks and flat rectangular stones.

There are many ways to irrigate a crop. In some areas most of the farmers use flood irrigation. This is done by tapping into a main irrigation canal, ditch, or flume and letting the water flow freely down the furrows. Also there are lots of different types of sprinkler systems. Sprinklers water the ground much like rain. Sometimes the farmer has sprinklers attached to pipes which are picked up manually and moved from one set to another. Some systems are on wheels. When the water has been in one spot long enough, one person can roll the wheels, with the pipe and sprinklers, forty feet or so to the next set. Then he connects it to the main line and waters that set.

There is also a big single sprinkler connected to a plastic pipe line rolled on a huge wheel mechanism. This is attached to the main line and unrolled to the end of the field and set to wind up at a speed to put on the right amount of water during the move.

Then there is a sprinkler system called the circle sprinkler. That source of water is in the middle of the field. A line is attached to it then rotates around the field on wheels irrigating the entire field. Of course it does not cover the corners of the field, but the convenience of it makes up for the dry corners. This type is popular in large grain areas where the fields are large and few people are required to farm many acres.

A drip system is another type of system. This has small holes located at the trunks of trees, vines, or plants. The water goes on slowly and only at those places. This way, the farmer can avoid any water loss by evaporation such as happens from a sprinkler. This is good for conserving water. It is especially adaptable to hillsides. It prevents erosion caused by water running downhill and taking the soil with it.

When the ground is irrigated, the weeds burst through within a few days. A green carpet covers the ground. It is a nuisance to the farmer and competes with the crop for moisture and nutrients. Again, there is the cycle of watering and then removing the unwanted vegetation, either by machine, hand labor, or chemicals.

There are also sprays and dust that can rid the crop of insects which are out to use the crop to satisfy their own wants. When they have invaded fields, farmers have lost crops that could have fed many people. There are soil-borne and air-borne pests which are ready to compete with the farmer for his crop. The farmer has to make a living for his family, and be able to repay the bank or other money source for the expense of growing and harvesting the crop. If he can not make a living at farming, he will be forced to move into another business, profession, or labor. So he uses the method which produces the most abundant crop with the least expense, the same as any businessman does.

# Chapter V

# Farm Animals

Long before recorded history of our land, there were people roaming the area hunting game for meat to eat for survival. A balanced diet for humans requires a large amount of protein. Animals contain a complete protein and have always been widely used for human food.

There were buffalo to feed many tribes of people. In early days, there were wild turkeys available for the taking. There were prairie chickens, wild pigs, sheep and wild goats, deer, antelope, elk, and many smaller animals such as rabbits and squirrels used for food. Their hides were used for clothing and shelter. Without these animals, the inhabitants of this land would have had a more difficult time surviving.

## Cattle

Raising beef cattle is a major farm enterprise. In some areas the ranchers have acres and acres of pasture, sometimes native grass, for their cattle to graze on. Some farmers have several pastures, and they alternate the cattle. When one pasture is

Horses grazing for their lunch.

Sheep making the most of the pasture.

Baby turkeys just out from the hatchery.

Adult turkeys around a very young farmer.

Beef cattle grazing on lush grass.

grazed down low, the rancher moves his herd onto a different one to give the first pasture grass an opportunity to grow again. Land that would not be too productive for growing other crops can still support cattle. The farmer gives his cattle hay, grain and properly mixed rations to supplement the pasture when needed. He always gives them extra rations when he wants to "top them off," fatten them for market. These rations include plenty of field corn. In other areas the cattle are in small pastures and are fed more hay and grains. Sometimes the animals are in the feed lot most of the time. By doing this, the farmer can get more steaks and hamburgers on many more tables per acre of ground available to him. These animals must have constant care and proper diet. The farmer also must see that they have certain shots to keep them healthy.

Some farmers raise their own grain and grind it for livestock feed. Others buy feed from the feed store and hay from other farmers who grow it. Some also feed silage. Silage is corn stalks (sometimes with ears of corn), grass or other green foliage that has been chopped and stored in some kind of air-tight storage and allowed to ferment before feeding.

In the Bible when the prodigal son returned home, the father ordered the servants to kill a fatted calf and prepare a feast to celebrate the occasion. This tells us that beef has been used for food for a very long time.

## Dairy Cows

Dairying is another major farm enterprise. A dairy is so specialized that a dairyman usually does little farming besides his dairy. He usually grows some hay, perhaps some grain, and something for silage, and pasture. He usually likes to have enough pasture to rotate his stock onto a different one every several days. The dairyman, though, converts all that he grows into feed for his stock. He must milk the cows at least twice a day—real early in the morning and again at evening time. There always must be someone on hand to do these chores twice, or more, every day all year long. He has little time to spend on other farming. If he grows some of his feed, he can cut costs, and that is important to all types of farming as well as any other business.

## Sheep

In Biblical times, sheep were very important to people. Today, these farm animals still fill certain needs of people. Sheep supply wool for our clothing, blankets, and rugs. They also furnish lamb chops and leg of lamb roasts for the dining tables.

Sheep are grazers and can nip a pasture to the ground. They are not adventurous animals by nature. They need a leader in their group, or need guarding, and driving by a herder or dogs. They require much care from the farmer. There is a lambing time when all the ewes give birth to the lambs. This has to be watched over especially well.

Just before lambing time the ewes are placed inside shelter to protect them from weather and wild animals such as coyotes. During lambing season there are many nights when the farmer gets very little sleep. He is out with the sheep to care for their needs. Sheep also need a proper diet. Their pasture food will be supplemented with other food when needed.

When the weather starts getting warm, the farmer relieves his sheep of their heavy coats. Usually he gets a group of shearers to come in and finish with the job as fast as possible. That is a busy time for him. This requires getting the animals penned, housed, and fed during the shearing.

### Goats

Goats are hardy animals and require less care than most farm livestock. Goats are browsers and are very helpful to a farmer who has cleared his ground of trees, but needs some help in keeping the young sprouts down. He must keep fences in good repair if he expects to keep his goats under control. They are good climbers and like high places. Most often the farmer has just enough goats for his own use.

In many other countries, more people drink milk from goats than they do from cows. Goat's milk also has a place in this country. It is widely used for infants and children who can not digest cow's milk or who may be allergic to it. Goat's milk is easier to digest. Older people also can use it when they are unable to use other milk.

Angora goats give us mohair for wooly sweaters and trim for garments. In this country, goat's meat is not eaten as much as in some other places. The meat has somewhat of a wild taste which many people dislike.

There are goat dairies in this country. Dairy goats require more work from the farmer. He has to milk them twice a day and have more shelter than for the ones he lets run out in the pasture all of the time. The milk goats need special feed to produce more milk.

## Poultry — Chickens

Practically everyone enjoys fried chicken. It goes well on a picnic and yet it is just as valuable in a formal dining room in a five-course dinner. The chicken farmer buys these birds just a day after hatching. They require special attention. They need nice warm brooders to gather around for warmth. They have a complete ration which is specially ground and mixed for them. They are given vitamin shots to keep them healthy. They are usually put in huge houses with controlled temperature, sterile environment, automatic watering and feeding equipment. The farmer normally requires anyone entering to disinfect his feet before he goes through the door. This is a very expensive set-up and some farmers do more of their work by hand labor than automatic machines. Either way, they keep a constant watch over the welfare of the birds. The birds are sold for fryers at about eight weeks old.

The laying hens are housed in large buildings with

plenty of nests. These buildings can be automated, or most of the work can be done with hand labor. In addition to our breakfast egg, there are many uses for this protein giving food. These chickens also require lots of attention, such as watering, feeding, temperature checking, and egg gathering. Also the farmer makes a careful check on the birds themselves to make sure they are in good physical condition.

**Turkeys**

Most often we think of turkeys as a Thanksgiving and Christmas dinner food. But there are a variety of good things from turkeys. We now have turkey hams, sausage and various types of meat in addition to a roasted bird for dinner.

This is a specialty crop and the turkey growers seldom do other farming on a large scale. They normally grow at least part of their feed, and some grind their own and store it on the farm where they will have easy access when it is needed. Turkey food is very delicately balanced to get the greatest benefit from it. In good weather, the turkeys are pastured outside. The farmer rotates the area frequently, giving them new pasture and a clean area in which to exercise. When turkeys are small, they are housed in large buildings with heat lamps for cold and fans for hot weather. In fact, when they are inside, the temperature is very critical. It must be watched constantly.

## Hogs

Hogs are another important farm animal. From them we get ham, bacon, and various fresh pork cuts. Field corn farming goes well with pig raising. The hogs use a large amount of corn for their diet. They have a well balanced diet consisting of different grains and additives to keep them healthy. They require special housing and much care to reach maturity, and bring in a profit to the farmer. Again, the farmer may grow and grind his feed and add the needed vitamins and minerals to keep his pigs in good condition and gaining weight at a constant rate. Some farmers have brood sows to grow their stock; others buy the pigs at a young age and then grow them out to market time. Hogs need special food and attention to give a good finished product. One can tell by checking the ham if a pig has had proper feed or if the farmer has skimped on his rations.

## Rabbits

Rabbits are animals which can furnish us a lot of good eating. A rabbit farmer can supply more meat per pound of feed than a cattle farmer. This of course makes the meat cheaper to the consumer and gives the farmer as much money above the cost of raising the animals as does any other animal. Their basic feed is ground alfalfa pellets with additives to assure a well balanced diet. In pioneering days the families ate lots of small game such as rabbits. They were easier to capture, especially in bad weather. Rabbit is a delicate tasting meat similar to chicken, but it has less bone for the amount of meat. The farmer must provide hutches, or cages, to house his animals. These contain dispensers for food and water and nesting beds for does. He has to give them a lot of attention, but he is rewarded with good produce.

In the past the rabbits have given fur to warm the hands, heads, and bodies of many cold American Indians and pioneers.

**Horses**

There was a time when horses were essential to farming. They pulled the plows, cultivators, and harvest machines. Horses also pulled the wagons which hauled the produce to market. Now there are more horses used for pleasure than work. They are still used in some areas for logging. A horse can go through mud that would stop a car or truck. Some police forces use horses for certain jobs. Ranchers still use horses to round up their cattle. They are especially good when a rancher moves his cattle down into a winter range area. The farmer must feed his horses regularly. Their usual diet is pasture, hay and ground grain. The farmer usually has plenty of pasture for his animals, and he probably will grow some of the feed. The farmer makes sure his horses have plenty of clean fresh water. Hay, grain and cattle work well as crops to grow along with horses.

The farmer must keep the fences repaired, and that is no easy job if he has a lot of acres in pasture. It is also a good policy to divide the pasture and let one part grow while another is being grazed. The stock need shelter from sun, rain and wind.

Another important thing for the horse farmer to do is see that his riding stock is ridden frequently. If left alone too long, some horses have a tendency to forget who is the master. They may decide not to follow instructions. A farmer might even find himself suddenly on the ground, instead of the comfortable saddle he was in a second earlier. That is, if the horse is of that temperament, and some of them are.

# Chapter VI

# Equipment and Shop

The farmer has a tremendous amount of money tied up in necessary farm equipment and shop tools. He not only has to put out a lot of dollars to purchase the machines, but he spends many more dollars and hours of labor keeping them in working condition. If a machine breaks down during harvest, and it is not repaired immediately and put back into the field, there could be an enormous loss of perishable fruits or vegetables. This would cut down on the farmer's income and deprive many people of that food to eat. In the United States the average farmer supplies the food for more than sixty people—enough to completely feed them.

Tilling equipment is important to most farmers. Practically all crops begin on tilled soil. There are many types of machines to do this work. Most of these were mentioned in chapter two. The farmer chooses the types that will suit his particular needs for the kind of crops he raises.

## Fertilizer and Spray Equipment

Most farmers own some kind of spray equipment.

Tandem discs are used to turn under weeds and other refuse.

An air-conditioned tractor.

Spraying young cherry trees.

Farm shops are often better equipped than commercial garages.

For orchard crops a farmer needs a different set-up than he does for row crops or ground-cover crops. There is a large tank with wide booms to cover a huge swath down the field, then there are those for rows and even individual plants or trees. The booms and blowers can sometimes be adjusted to do several different jobs. There are big blowers that can cover an orchard tree to prevent the worms from eating the fruit before the farmer has an opportunity to harvest it.

There are different fertilizer machines. There are those which scatter it in the rows, also those that insert it in the ground. To get the most from his soil the farmer needs to use some of these.

### Planting Equipment

The farmer must have a planter for each type of crop he grows. These can be changed to cover several different crops, but not for different types. Many different crops which are grown from seeds can be planted using the same planter after some changes have been made. Among these are green beans, dry beans, field corn, and sweet corn. Grains such as wheat, rye, oats, barley and rice, and grass need another type of planter. A nursery-tree stock planter is different from other plant machines, but some plant crop planters such as those for strawberries and cabbage are interchangeable.

### Cultivating Equipment

The majority of farmers use some type of

cultivating machinery. The type depends on the crops they grow. Tillers, cultivators with various shovels are used, along with hand tools such as hoes and rakes. Some crops need the soil turned into the row around the crop, and some want the dirt pulled away from the plants. Still others need to have the ground stirred and leveled between the rows. Some need different things done at different times. Nursery stock growers eliminate the weeds by going through their young tree rows with cultivators.

**Foraging Equipment**

A hay farmer needs a mowing machine, raking and windrowing machine, baler, and loading equipment if he plans to bale and store his crop. Or he may choose a chopper that chops it in the field, then it is trucked to a silage storage and preserved for later use. There is also a cubing machine that makes pellets for feed. Grass, clover, and alfalfa are the most common hay crops. Silage can be made from these, or from any green edible fodder.

**Harvesting Equipment**

In Biblical times the method used to "combine" (or harvest) the grain was to throw the grain into the air and let the wind blow away the chaff while the grain fell back to the catch basket. Of course they usually had to wait until evening when the wind was strong enough to separate these. They also had to do some beating on the grain to get the husk off before they could do the separating. Our methods have changed considerably.

Combines are machines used for wheat and all kinds of other grains. The farmer must invest in other headers for his combine so that he can convert it from one crop to another. This sometimes means he spends several thousand dollars for these conversions parts in addition to many hours labor for the changes. Combines are also used for dry beans, clover seed, grass seed, alfalfa, sugar beet seed, and field corn.

Some tomatoes are mechanically harvested. Some are still hand picked. Potatoes, beets, carrots, and sugar beets each have a similar, but specialized harvester. Green beans and peas have similar harvesters. There are harvest-helps for hand harvested crops to speed up the harvest and cut down on the expense. Cabbage, cantaloupe, and lettuce are among those with aids. Sometimes the farmer machine-harvests some fruit. This bruises the fruit more than normal hand picking so the grower usually blends the two methods. For fresh market he hand picks and for cannery or processing he uses machines. A fruit and nut tree harvester is a massive catch frame and shaker large enough to shake the entire tree. This type harvest works for walnuts, pecans, almonds, prunes, and cherries. Filberts fall free off the trees. The farmer then uses sweepers and blowers to get the nuts from under the trees and out in the middle where the harvester picks them up and sends them into a trailer or tote box. The hand equipment the farmer needs for his hand harvest crops are buckets, harnesses for hanging the buckets onto the persons for easy handling, and ladders for tree fruit.

The farmer needs trucks galore to haul his produce to market, cannery, wholesale house, or storage. Most of the year they are headed to the farm, they bring the seed, fertilizer, plants, and all materials he will need, but at the end of the season they are busy hauling produce away from the farm. Most progressive farmers like to trade their old equipment every few years, that is if there have been many helpful changes. They should be sure they can justify this by saving more crops or doing a job more efficiently, because this is an expensive trade.

Loading equipment is important for many crops. Some farmers use tractors with loaders attached. Others have a hyster type machine, which is a complete loading machine, that can lift totes and pallets onto trucks for hauling to whatever outlet the farmer uses to sell his product.

A farmer normally needs several tractors because of their many uses. He uses them to pull, push, dig and lift. Tractors tow the planters that make those straight rows of seeds or plants through the fields. Sometimes with the aid of a loader attached, the machine lifts big totes or pallets of vegetables, fruits or nuts onto trucks. With the aid of a power auger, tractors dig the holes for fence posts, posts for berry fields, and holes to plant orchard trees. With a bulldozer blade attached in front, tractors push the dirt over the cliff or up a hill, or make a dam to keep water out of the field. They also can dig a ditch to drain unwanted water. With a blade attached to the rear, the machines grade the farm roads. They pull some of the harvesters or harvest aids, and also take a hungry farmer to his house for lunch.

The animal farmers usually have less farm equipment. Their money is tied up in fencing, housing, and the dairymen have a huge amount of money invested in milking parlors and milking machines.

Now with the picture of all the machinery required to do a good job of farming a normal farm, one can easily see that there would be a lot of shop tools and work to repair and maintain these things. The shop tools consist of a drill press, hoist, grinder, welders, lathe, and various hand tools. The farmers vary in the degree of work they do on their own equipment. Some have very modern well-equipped shops and do the major overhauls in addition to small repairs. Others hire someone to do the work, but most farmers do some of their upkeep. During the off season a wise farmer goes over each of the machines to be sure that he replaces the worn and broken parts. He does everything he can to ready the machines for their part as this big scene unfolds into a major food basket operation.

*Chapter VII*

# Harvest

Harvest is one of the most rewarding times for the farmer. At this time he can see the fruits of his entire year's labor. If he has been alert all year, and performed the needed operations—and if the weather has co-operated, the farmer should make money to live on for a while. It is a thrill to see those rose-cheeked peaches on the trees ready for harvest. A farmer knows he is largely responsible for their quality and quantity.

A farmer standing by a field of waving amber grain may be reminded of a huge sea of hot butter-scotch topping rippled by a giant blowing it.

He may even see the green corn standing in a field as a big forest full of hidden treasures. This is true as one realizes when the picker or truck comes out of the field with a load of edible golden kernels. The farmer spends little time in dreaming, though, because of the many things to get ready and coordinate for the harvest.

There are several different ways of harvesting crops. In just a few days he can get acres and acres of grain harvested, but it requires weeks and lots of

A grain storage elevator.

(Above) A sugar cane harvester.
(Below) Strawberries ready for market.

A young man operating an intricate harvesting machine.

labor to harvest a few acres of strawberries.

For grain, soy beans, dry beans, grass seed, and many seed crops a farmer can harvest his crop with a huge machine, trucks, and only a few men. The harvest can continue until it is completed, that is, after the crop dries out each morning until it starts getting damp in the evening. The combines and trucks are expensive machines, though.

Cannery and processing crops are different in that the farmer must coordinate his output with the amount the processor can handle at a given time. For mechanically harvested cannery crops the harvesting continues on a twenty-four-hour basis while the cannery is running. A particular harvest crew might be in the field any time day or night. The farmer must have a harvester, truck, and men to operate them when the plant needs the product. The cannery field-man gives the growers orders for the product needed from him between what hours.

Machine harvest is the only thing which keeps down the cost of food. Green beans, sweet corn, peas, beets, and carrots are among the mechanically harvested vegetable cannery crops.

Squash, broccoli, cauliflower, asparagus, and cucumbers are among those which use hand labor to harvest. But the farmer provides aids such as conveyors at a low level to take the product up and into totes or trailers. There are various helps to assist hand laborers to do the harvest job more efficiently, and with less strenuous labor. Some farmers have tried pulling low platforms covering several rows and allowing persons to sit or lie on them while picking the crop.

Because of the drudgery of hand harvest, most of the crops are machine harvested. There are still some which engineers or farmers have been unable to devise a machine that harvests efficiently. They either bruise the crop too much or lose too much of it. Where there are multiple fruit or vegetables on one plant they seldom all ripen at the same time. If the farmer comes through the field with a harvester which cuts the vine or bush, and then picks the product, there would be some overripe while others would be green. Perhaps there would be those barely past bloom stage. The farmer would be paid a normal rate for the mature or prime crop. He would receive much less or nothing for the overripe, and the green would be a total loss. When crops are hand harvested they are picked more than one time each season. Even a harvester which doesn't damage the plant picks all the product on the plant. Building a harvester that distinguishes between green and ripe costs too much. That puts the machine beyond the price range for practical use.

Men are trying to improve the species of plants to make them more adaptable to mechanical harvesting. They have propagated qualities into many plants that make them more productive and more adaptable to the farmer's needs. They have improved the taste and holding quality of many.

Most strawberries, trailing and cane berries are hand picked. They require buses and cars loaded

Filberts (hazel nuts).

Harvesting boysenberries.

Harvesting cauliflower.

Consumers enjoying corn-on-the-cob.

Combining grain.

Picking peaches for fresh market.

Harvesting sweet corn.

Harvesting yellow squash.

with people to harvest the crop before the berries get overripe. In some areas school kids over twelve can still earn some money for school clothes while enjoying each other's company, plus doing a service for the farmer as they pick the berries. Anytime the farmer has a crew of laborers doing the hand harvesting, he must have ticket punchers to keep track of each youngster's output. He needs loaders to continue a flow of berries going onto the truck. Then it is ready for him when he needs to go to the cannery or market.

Some raspberries and some blackberries are harvested with a vibrating device which shakes the berries off the vine onto a wide canvas belt which conveys them into crates. This requires someone changing crates as they are filled. This operation is rough on the fruit, though. It is good for processing into jam, but it is not the best for freezing whole berries. There are too many crushed by the vibration and the drop. Cherries and some other tree-fruit are harvested by shaking and catching, but again it is too rough for some uses. The farmer must have a large crew to harvest his apples, pears, peaches, and apricots by hand. A picker will put on a picking harness with a bucket, and sometimes he needs to climb a ladder to reach the fruit. The smaller trees are now more popular for some orchard fruits. They are called semi-dwarf trees. While the harvest is going on, the farmer is hauling fruit to cannery or processor, and depositing boxes all through the orchard for the pickers. He also must see that drinking water is available for the laborers. He makes sure his helpers have adequate toilets in the orchard area.

Carrots, beets, sugar beets, and potatoes are among the root crops which must have a digging harvester. The machines separate the tops from the crop and move the crop into a hopper, trailer, or truck.

Fresh market carrots and beets would need more hand labor. The farmer would dig them with a digger that leaves the tops attached. Then people would pick, wash and bunch them.

Potatoes are mechanically harvested. This operation requires several persons riding on the harvester, throwing dirt clods off the machine. Otherwise the grower might end up with a warehouse half full of field dirt.

Among crops that require the hand laborers to use knives are cauliflower, asparagus, broccoli, rhubarb, and cabbage. The farmer must have a supply of knives available for the people doing the harvesting.

Cucumbers are hand harvested with aids to help. Their harvest season continues over several weeks. The farmer sometimes abandons his field not because there can be no more to pick, but he has fulfilled his contracts. He discontinues the irrigation. If he has time he then discs the field to put the vines back into the ground to start the plant breakdown for the benefit of future crops.

The nurseryman digs his fruit trees with a huge digger especially equipped to do the job. This requires many people to pick up the dug trees then tie them in bundles in order to handle them. They are placed onto trailers and brought into storage where they will be graded later. But they will be ready for the orchardist when the time comes to plant trees in a new orchard.

Cotton is picked with a large machine. It throws the cotton up and into a wire cage on the picker. Then the cotton is dumped along the edge of the field and squeezed into huge trailersize blocks to await time to move into the gin for processing.

Most animal farmers do their harvesting by taking their product to processing plants. From there it is distributed in many ways to the consumer. Some farmers sell a portion of their produce directly to the consumer. These livestock farmers do their harvest throughout the year. They gather their eggs daily. They grow more than one crop of frying chickens, rabbits, or turkeys. Lots and lots of turkeys are sold for Thanksgiving and Christmas dinners. Beef is more of a once-a-year harvest. Pork is usually sold two or three times annually. Dairymen harvest daily. Milking, whether it is goats or cows, is a daily operation.

But harvest time is the farmer's time of collecting his produce in readiness for marketing. It is a time of rejoicing or weeping—depending on whether his crop is good or bad and the price is high or low.

# Chapter VIII

# Processing

There are many ways of processing food. The Indians used a mortar and pestle to grind their grain for bread. As a result of this method of grinding, their teeth wore down considerably due to the sand from the two stone instruments mixing with the ground grain. Our processing has changed.

We still grind our grain but it is usually done in a large mill which substitutes stainless steel equipment for the Indian's stone grinders. Some of the grains are ground as a coarse finished product for animal food. Some are ground a little finer for cereals. Some end up as a meal type product. Last, there is the powder type which is the flour for bread. Then, of course, more than one grind can be mixed to add texture to foods.

A large portion of our foods are canned. Canning is suitable for preserving vegetables such as beans, peas, asparagus, carrots, beets, spinach, and tomatoes. Just about every fruit is good canned. Canning is a matter of cleansing the fruit or vegetables, dicing, slicing, chopping, or leaving whole, then placing them in the cans, then adding salt to the vegetables and meats, then sealing the cans, and cooking the product for the required time.

Fruit usually has sugar syrup added before cooking. Some sweet fruits are canned in their own type juice without any sugar. Canning is a good way to preserve juices for later use. Tomato is the leading vegetable juice. There are more fruits than vegetables made into juice.

Green beans, among other vegetables, are dumped onto a concrete slab or receiving bays outside the cannery building, then pushed into a conveyor by a forklift with a scoop which takes a huge bite out of the stack as it pushes. They go through a dirt reel which permits small beans and dirt to fall through the holes. A suction fan removes the loose leaves. Then cutting knives cut the beans off the vines. Then they are washed. A snipper removes the ends and stems. They are then cut into desired sizes, the large ones are usually sliced into French cut. They are placed in cans and cooked. After cooking, cooling, and adding labels, they are stored. During these operations there are many inspections to insure a good product.

Freezing is another favorite method of keeping food for later use. One is able to freeze almost anything. In some areas the canneries start their freezing process season with strawberries. They are brought into the plant, then dumped from the crates onto a conveyor which takes them through a water spray to cleanse them. They are then individually quick frozen or they are sliced and sugar is added, then placed in cartons and frozen. They are stored until consumers want them. Stone fruits such as peaches, apricots, and prunes require another step to prepare them for freezing. Their pits and cores must be removed and most of them are peeled.

Corn is a vegetable which is brought to the freezing plant and dumped onto a slab then scooped into the conveyor for the entrance into the plant. The first operation is into the husker where the corn husk is removed, then it travels through a washer and water spray which takes the silks away. The line divides and those ears which will make nice corn-on-the-cob are frozen after both ends have been cut off, so that the ears will be the same size. The kernels are cut off for kernel corn, then it is frozen. After freezing it is packaged and stored until ordered for a consumer.

Many other vegetables are frozen. They are basically done the same way but the preparation is different for different things. The basic freezing method though, is clean, freeze, package, and store. Beets, carrots, broccoli, and many other vegetables are chopped, sliced, diced, cut into one inch pieces, or left whole. All vegetables must be blanched, that is, cooked, before they are frozen. That is to kill the enzymes which would prevent them from keeping. After cooking, these vegetables are cooled in chilling water before they go onto the freezing belt.

The canneries and freezing plants process produce while they are fresh to insure the very best flavor and quality. This means the farmer can not pick and deliver it to the plant until the canneries are

Corn at a freezer plant.

A turkey round-up.

Waxing tomatoes.

Canning green beans.

ready to process it.

Cucumbers, cabbage, various relishes, some other vegetables, fruits, and meats are pickled to preserve. Practically everyone likes a nice pickle slice or some relish on a hamburger. Sauerkraut goes well with wieners or a reuben sandwich.

Preserving with sugar is another way of using fruits for something good. Jelly, jam, marmalade, and apple and pear butter, when spread on toast turns it into a special treat.

Drying is another method of preserving fruit, vegetables, and meats. In Illinois at Koster Site dig, archaeologists found that back in 3500 B.C. the Indians had large fish drying racks they used to preserve their food. This method has been in practice a very long time.

The plants dry the products while they are fresh and plentiful, then have them available when they are not so easy to get. During the long cold winter it is nice to have as much variety as possible. Among fruits that are often dried are prunes, apricots, peaches, pears, and apples. The vegetables which are dried most regularly are onions, green pepper, soup mixes, and potatoes. These can be freeze-dried or dried with heat and fan circulation. There are special driers for many fruits and nuts. The freezing plants which freeze the fruits and vegetables do the freeze-drying. One of the winter crops which help keep the processing plants going is potatoes. They freeze many of the French fries that we eat with our hamburgers, fish and chips, and other foods.

After the blades are removed from the sugar cane, the juice is squeezed from the stalks. Sugar beets are bulbs that supply juice for beet sugar. The juice is cooked and condensed into sugar.

Animals are usually taken to a processing plant. More beef is used fresh; it is cut into various cuts such as roasts, steaks, and ground for hamburgers or the many ways ground meat is used. There is some that is seasoned, smoked, and processed for weiners, cold cuts, and other types such as that. Some beef is dried and some is frozen. Some is canned, some is mixed with other foods and canned or frozen. Most TV dinners have meat as a main course.

Pork is used fresh. Also it is smoked and cured as hams or bacon. It is ground for sausage. Some is canned and still a considerable amount is mixed with other foods, then canned or frozen.

Turkeys, chickens, and rabbits are used fresh for frying or roasting, and sometimes ground for patties. Turkeys especially are used for hams, smoked and chopped in many varieties of lunch meats and weiners. These meats are also canned and frozen.

Sheep are used fresh for lamb chops, stew meat, or roasts. Goats are used fresh. Many times there is a barbecue feed with the goat being barbecued.

Milk is taken to a dairy processing operation where it is cartoned as milk, cream, or half-and-half. Butter is made from the cream. Some of the cream becomes the sour cream many persons like on baked potatoes. There are many other ways to use it. Some milk ends up as cheese. While some more of it becomes cottage cheese. Yogurt is a popular milk food.

Eggs are mostly used fresh. Some are dried for packaged cakes, pudding mixes, and many other packaged foods. Some are frozen to be used later. Eggs are usually separated before freezing—whites and yolks are frozen separately. Bakeries use a lot of frozen eggs in their baking.

# Chapter IX

# **Sales and Marketing**

By 1500 B.C. the Indians were marketing their surplus corn along with all the things they had made and gathered. They would load these in their dugout canoes and go on the river course. They visited all the villages along the river and traded the items they had brought for those the natives had to trade. They spent several weeks on these journeys. By this means they could get rid of the surplus, and bring needed things home for their families to use. Among the trading items of that day were animal skins for clothing and shelter, feathers for decorations, and tools they had made from rocks and sticks. Some areas had shells and turquoise for jewelry. The variety of trading items helped everyone to live a more rounded life. The same is true today, but we do our marketing in a little different way.

## Canning and Freezing

There are several ways of marketing and many different outlets. One of the most common ways for row crop farmers to sell his crops is to a local cannery. Many canneries either can or freeze the

Packing peaches for the fresh market.

A farmer's roadside produce stand.

products. Before planting time the farmer contacts the cannery to find out how much of his crops he can contract to them. He plants accordingly. He may do other type marketing in addition to selling to the cannery, but this is considered in his overall planning. This applies only to the fruits and vegetables which one can freeze or can. Other chapters have given examples of those which can be treated in this manner.

This type marketing would entail harvesting and hauling to the plant. There they would weigh and grade it and the farmer would be paid different prices for various grades. It is a simple way of marketing specific types of crops.

**Fresh Market**

Another way, and one in which the farmer stands to make more profit, is in fresh market. This is a more detailed and complicated way of marketing a crop. This means the farmer not only must harvest his crop, but he must do a variety of steps to prepare it for marketing. Radishes, carrots, green onions, and many other vegetables which are fresh marketed are washed, bunched, or packed in small plastic bags, ready for the grocer to place on his display stand. Many vegetables such as asparagus and broccoli, in addition to being washed, must be trimmed to a uniform size after bunching. Most of these vegetables are packed in crates and sold by the crates to wholesale houses, stores, stands, or brokers who do the selling to consumer outlets.

Fresh market sweet corn is harvested, sometimes by hand, other times with a mechanical picker. It is then brought into a packing plant where it is graded, packed into crates, and sent through a refrigerated tank to cool the corn immediately. This prevents the sugar from turning to starch. Sometimes it is sent through the tank before packing. The cooling retains the sweet flavor and extends the keeping quality for a few days.

Peaches, pears, and apples are among the fruits which are graded according to size and packed in boxes for market. Peaches must be moved immediately before they ripen too much. Pears are usually stored for a while to let them ripen. They must be picked before they are fully ripe so they will not fall to the ground. They fall before they are ripe. They are placed in storage and taken to market as they ripen. Some apples are also stored in controlled temperature storage and sold through the winter. For these, the farmer needs a controlled air storage building.

Tomatoes and cucumbers are among the fresh vegetables which are sometimes sent through a waxing machine to add luster to their skins. This in turn adds eye appeal when the buyer enters the store to make the purchase. As a nation, the United States citizens feel they want to see beauty in everything. They also want things done up in plastic bags or some kind of easy handling package. They look for convenience in almost everything. The farmer tries to please by supplying what the public seems to want.

Potatoes are harvested with a mechanical harvester. If he wants to market these as fresh market produce and do his own selling, the work does not stop there. He must have a large storage warehouse, plus washing and sorting equipment. Then his crew can spend most of the winter months grading and bagging potatoes for local stores and wholesale houses. There are many sizes to use in grading the potatoes. French friers, bakers, and a smaller size for some household customers. Some businesses like one size for the bakers they serve on their dinners, while other eating places prefer another size for their customers. The wise farmer tries to be ready with the right sizes for all needs.

## Fruit and Vegetable Stands

Many farmers have stands where they sell the fruit and vegetables they grow. Usually this is a good way to market for a small farmer, perhaps a farmer who has not sold his entire crop to the cannery. If he has not contracted his whole crop, or he has a surplus after his sales to wholesale houses, this is another outlet for his produce which usually makes money for him. He tries to have all the variety possible for the area. If he does not raise most of the available produce in the area, he sometimes buys from other nearby growers. Most people living near enough to drive out enjoy the drive, and appreciate the fresh produce. The farmer must have a crew picking and packing the produce to keep plenty available. There is always someone doing the selling at the stand. This is an outlet that has been popular in some areas.

## U-Pick

Another way of marketing a crop is through U-pick. The farmer grows it and gets it ready for harvest then advertises it for U-pick. The interested people come out and pick what they want of fresh produce for canning, freezing, or just to have an abundance of fresh produce to eat for a while. The grower can either advertise in the local newspaper or radio station. He may have done this for so long that enough people know about it. To sell his crops, he depends on his satisfied customers. The farmer usually has a sign near his farm directing customers to his stand. This type of harvest can cause some problems. One has to be careful not to damage the fruit trees or next year's fruit spurs when U-picking tree fruits. There must be ample supervision in this work. Also the grower must have something enticing enough to lure the public out to pick the produce. Many people like to do their own picking to be sure of the ripeness or just the type of produce they want at that particular time. The farmer usually requires the people to pick all the ripe produce as far as they pick. The U-picker takes only what he feels is good though. A U-picker usually checks the quality carefully. Strawberries, broccoli, pole beans, cucumbers, tomatoes, peaches, and apples are among those that work well for U-picking. If family members have time to pick the needed produce it is a big saving to the family, and they are assured it is fresh from the vine or tree. It can work well for everyone involved.

## Grains and Seed Crops

Grains and seed crops are delivered to grain companies for storage. Then it is sold by them when the farmer thinks the price is right for the sale. Or perhaps when the farmer needs his money for something. When it is sold to the grain warehouse, the farmer harvests it and hauls it in a bulk truck, then dumps it into the storage elevators. Many farmers now have their own storage. These are usually large steel circular buildings or bins which hold many tons of grain. The farmers who have these sometimes have their own cleaners, in order to get the trash and weed seed out as much as possible. Most weed seed is a different size from the grain, it will clean out fairly well. Care must be used to see that the seed is clean. Another farmer buying the seed does not appreciate having his field of wheat spotted with weeds from the seed he has just purchased. Grain exporting is very important to the United States. It helps balance the payments of manufactured goods we import from other countries.

These are some of the ways the farmers grow the products that feed this nation and help other nations as well.

# Glossary

**aeration** - air circulating through the ground
**converts** - changes
**cultigens** - cultivated crops not growing in the wild
**dormancy** - live but not actually growing, resting
**economic trouble** - money shortage
**eliminate** - omit, get rid of
**essential** - absolutely necessary
**extensively** - wide-spread, cover large area
**fertile** - able to produce a good crop
**germination** - seed sprouting
**humus** - vegetation of some sort which rots in the ground and improves it
**infectious** - a disease that spreads from one plant to another
**neutralize** - to add elements into the soil to cut down on the active parts of acid or alkali, to make it right for a particular need
**nutrients** - food
**penetrates** - goes into, roots punch holes in the ground and grow down
**perishable** - does not remain in good condition long, spoils
**potential** - the possible yield of fruit or vegetable if everything goes well
**primarily** - mostly
**propagated** - increase and improve their planting stock
**saturated** - soaked with water
**strenuous** - hard
**superior** - better
**susceptible** - easily affected with, unable to cope with certain conditions
**totes** - boxes for hauling cannery crops
**trenching** - making a ditch then placing tile (pipe) in it then covering it with soil

# References

*America's Fascinating Indian Heritage*
*The World of the American Indian*